Introducing the ultimate healthy pasta recipes book for kids! This book is jam-packed with delicious, nutritious, and easy-to-follow pasta recipes that are perfect for kids of all ages. With this book, you can rest easy knowing that your kids are enjoying delicious pasta dishes that are not only tasty but also good for them.

Inside the pages of this book, you'll find a wide variety of pasta recipes that are sure to satisfy even the pickiest of eaters. From classic favorites like spaghetti and meatballs to unique creations like pesto zucchini noodles, there's something for everyone in this book.

Each recipe has been carefully crafted to be both healthy and delicious. You'll find recipes that are low in fat, high in fiber, and packed with protein to keep your kids full and satisfied. Plus, many of the recipes feature fresh veggies and other nutritious ingredients that your kids might not even realize they're eating!

But that's not all - this book also includes helpful tips for getting your kids involved in the cooking process. From measuring ingredients to stirring the sauce, your little ones will love helping out in the kitchen and learning new cooking skills.

Whether you're a busy parent looking for quick and easy meal ideas or a health-conscious parent who wants to ensure their kids are eating well, this healthy pasta recipes book for kids is the perfect solution. So why not give it a try and start cooking up some healthy, tasty pasta dishes today!

Lemon Pasta

Ingredients

8 oz. package pasta (any long noodle)
2 - 3 tablespoons vegan butter or olive oil.
3 garlic cloves, minced.
1/4 teaspoon red pepper flakes, or to taste.
2 - 3 lemons (about 1/4 - 1/2 cup), juice of and some zest.
1/4 cup parsley, chopped.
salt & pepper, to taste.

If you're looking for a healthy and delicious pasta dish, this vegan Lemon Pasta is the perfect recipe for you. It's quick and easy to prepare, using simple ingredients like vegan butter or olive oil, minced garlic, red pepper flakes, lemons (juice of and zest), parsley, salt & pepper.

This dish is healthy, flavorful, and sure to impress!

To begin, cook the pasta according to the package instructions. Meanwhile, heat a large skillet over medium heat. Add in vegan butter or olive oil, garlic and red pepper flakes. Cook until fragrant and the garlic has softened slightly (about 1 minute). Stir in the lemon juice and zest and cook for an additional minute.

Drain the cooked pasta and add it to the skillet. Add in parsley, salt & pepper to taste, stirring until combined. Serve the lemon pasta warm with extra red pepper flakes, if desired. Enjoy!

Creamy Mushroom Pasta

Ingredients

8 ounces fettuccine pasta.
2 tablespoons olive oil.
¾ pound fresh white mushrooms, sliced.
¼ pound fresh shiitake mushrooms, stemmed and sliced.
salt and ground black pepper to taste.
2 cloves garlic, minced.
2 fluid ounces sherry.
1 cup chicken stock.

If you're looking for delicious recipes for kids, this creamy mushroom pasta is sure to please. With just a few ingredients and some simple steps, you can have an amazing dinner on your table in no time!

To start, bring a large pot of lightly salted water to a boil over high heat. Add the fettuccine pasta and cook for 8 to 10 minutes, or until al dente. Drain the pasta and set aside.

Next, heat the olive oil in a large skillet over medium-high heat. Add the mushrooms, season with salt and pepper, and sauté for 5 minutes. Reduce the heat to low, add the garlic and sherry, and cook for another 2 minutes.

Finally, add the chicken stock and bring to a boil. Once boiling, reduce heat to low and simmer for 5 minutes. Add the cooked fettuccine pasta and stir until the sauce coats the noodles evenly. Serve warm and enjoy!

This delicious mushroom pasta is sure to be a hit with kids of all ages. With its creamy sauce and delicious mushrooms, it's sure to become a family favorite. So don't wait any longer - try this delicious recipe today!

Bon Appétit!

Super Green Spaghetti

Ingredients

400g all-natural green spaghetti (made with dried spinach, zucchini, parsley, broccoli, and kale)
2 tablespoons extra-virgin olive oil
4 garlic cloves, minced
1/4 teaspoon red pepper flakes (optional)
2 cups fresh spinach leaves, packed
1/2 cup fresh parsley leaves, packed
1/4 cup fresh basil leaves, packed
1/4 cup fresh mint leaves, packed
1/4 cup pine nuts, toasted
1/2 cup grated Parmesan cheese
Salt and pepper, to taste

Instructions:

Cook the green spaghetti in a large pot of boiling salted water according to the package instructions until al dente. Reserve 1 cup of the pasta cooking water, then drain the spaghetti.

While the pasta is cooking, heat the olive oil in a large skillet over medium heat. Add the minced garlic and red pepper flakes (if using) and sauté for 1-2 minutes, until fragrant.

Add the spinach, parsley, basil, and mint to the skillet and cook, stirring occasionally, until the greens are wilted and tender, about 5 minutes.

In a blender or food processor, combine the cooked greens, toasted pine nuts, and grated Parmesan cheese. Process until the mixture forms a smooth paste.

Add the green paste to the skillet and stir until well combined. If the sauce seems too thick, add some of the reserved pasta cooking water to thin it out to your desired consistency.

Add the cooked spaghetti to the skillet and toss to coat with the sauce. Season with salt and pepper to taste.

Serve the Super Green Spaghetti hot, with additional grated Parmesan cheese and toasted pine nuts on top. Enjoy your delicious and healthy meal!

Chicken Alfredo Pasta

Chicken Alfredo Pasta is a classic Italian recipe that makes the perfect healthy lunch for kids. The creamy sauce, made with Parmesan and Romano cheese, is sure to be a hit with both children and adults alike.

To get started, begin by gathering your ingredients: 1 large boneless/skinless chicken breast (or 2 small ones), 6 tablespoons of salted butter (high quality is recommended), 3 cloves of garlic minced, 2 tablespoons all-purpose flour, 3 cups of half and half (half cream/half milk), ¾ cup Parmesan cheese grated, ½ cup Romano cheese grated, salt and black pepper to taste.

Once you have all the necessary ingredients, it's time to get cooking! Begin by seasoning the chicken on both sides with salt and pepper. Heat a large skillet over medium-high heat, then add 3 tablespoons of the butter. Once melted, add in the chicken and cook for 4-5 minutes per side or until cooked all the way through. Once cooked, transfer to a plate and set aside.

Next, reduce the heat to medium and add in the remaining 3 tablespoons butter. Once melted, stir in the garlic and cook for about 1 minute or until fragrant. Now, whisk in the flour and cook for an additional 1-2 minutes or until the mixture starts to lightly brown.

Then, slowly pour in the half and half while continuously whisking the mixture until fully combined. Bring the sauce to a simmer and let it cook for 4-5 minutes or until thickened, stirring occasionally. Now add in both cheeses, Parmesan and Romano, stirring until melted and fully combined.

Finally, add in the cooked chicken and any juice from the plate and stir until fully combined. Let simmer for an additional 1-2 minutes or until heated through. Serve over pasta with extra Parmesan cheese if desired. Enjoy!

This delicious Chicken Alfredo Pasta recipe is sure to be a hit with all your family and friends. It's a great way to enjoy a classic Italian dish while keeping your meal healthy and nutritious. Make it today for the perfect lunch or dinner!

Enjoy!

Chicken And Bacon Pasta

Ingredients needed
- boneless skinless chicken breast.
- smoked pancetta lardons (or bacon)
- chicken stock (made from a stock cube)
- parsley.
- garlic.
- onion.
- double cream.
- pasta shells.

Are you looking for delicious recipes that the whole family can enjoy? Look no further than this delicious chicken and bacon pasta! This delicious dish is perfect for picky eaters, and it's easy to make too. To get started, you'll need boneless skinless chicken breast, smoked pancetta lardons (or bacon), chicken stock (made from a stock cube), parsley, garlic, onion, double cream and some pasta shells.

Once you have all the ingredients ready to go, it's time to start cooking! Begin by heating up some butter or oil in a large saucepan over medium heat. Once the butter is melted, add the lardons and cook until golden. Add the garlic and onion to the pan, cooking for about 2 minutes until fragrant. Then add in the chicken breast and cook for 4-5 minutes, stirring occasionally.

Next, add the chicken stock to the pan and bring it to a gentle simmer before adding in the cream and parsley. Stir everything together and reduce the heat to low. Let the sauce simmer for about 10-15 minutes until it has reduced and thickened.

Finally, add in your cooked pasta shells and stir them through the sauce. Serve hot with a sprinkle of parsley on top and enjoy! With this delicious chicken and bacon pasta recipe, you'll have a meal that kids and adults will love. Enjoy!

Roasted Eggplant Pasta

Ingredients
1 large eggplant, cut into cubes.
1 small yellow onion, chopped (or half of a large onion)
1-2 Tablespoons oil.
1/2 teaspoon garlic powder.
2-3 cups tomato sauce.
1 16 oz. box of pasta noodles (see notes)
salt & black peppers.
fresh basil *optional.

This healthy roasted eggplant pasta dish is the perfect way to enjoy a cozy meal on any night of the week. Using just a few simple ingredients, this Italian-inspired dish comes together quickly and easily for an impressive dinner that's sure to please.

To begin, preheat your oven to 400 degrees Fahrenheit. Place the cubed eggplant on a baking sheet and drizzle it with oil. Sprinkle the garlic powder and salt & pepper over top, then give the eggplant cubes a good stir to evenly coat them with the seasonings. Roast in the oven for 30-35 minutes until lightly browned and tender.

Meanwhile, prepare your pasta noodles according to the package instructions. When cooked, drain and set aside.

In a large skillet or Dutch oven, heat the remaining oil over medium-high heat. Add in the chopped onion and cook for 5 minutes or until softened. Add in the tomato sauce and stir to combine. Once bubbling, reduce heat to low and simmer for 10 minutes.

Add the roasted eggplant and cooked pasta noodles to the sauce and stir to combine. Simmer everything together for 3-5 minutes, then remove from heat. Serve with a sprinkle of fresh basil, if desired. Enjoy!

Pomodoro Sauce

Ingredients

5 pounds peeled fresh tomatoes or 3 28-ounce cans of San Marzano whole peeled tomatoes.
2 tablespoons olive oil.
½ peeled and finely minced/grated yellow onion.
4 finely minced/grated garlic cloves.
12-15 fresh basil leaves.
sea salt and pepper to taste.
cooked pasta.

Pomodoro pasta is a healthy and delicious dish to make at home. It's simple to prepare and requires just a few fresh ingredients.

To begin, heat the olive oil in a large saucepan over high heat. Once it's hot, add the onion and garlic, cooking until fragrant - about three minutes. Then, add the tomatoes and all seasonings. Simmer for 15-20 minutes, stirring occasionally to prevent burning. Once the sauce is thickened and reduced, reduce the heat and add the fresh basil leaves.

Meanwhile, cook your pasta according to package instructions until al dente (it will finish cooking in the sauce). Drain in and add to the pomodoro sauce, stirring until everything is well combined. Season with more salt and pepper if desired.

Enjoy your healthy home-cooked pomodoro pasta! Serve it alone or topped with freshly grated Parmesan cheese. Enjoy!

Pesto Pasta

Ingredients

6 ounces spaghetti, reserve 1/2 cup starchy pasta water.
1/3 to 1/2 cup. basil pesto or vegan pesto.
Extra-virgin olive oil, for drizzling.
Fresh lemon juice, as desired.
4 cups arugula.
2 tablespoons pine nuts.
Pinches of red pepper flakes.
Sea salt and freshly ground black pepper.

Pesto pasta is a great way to make a healthy, delicious lunch for the kids. Start by boiling your spaghetti in salted water according to the package instructions. Once cooked, reserve about 1/2 cup of starchy boiled pasta water before draining.

In a separate bowl, mix together basil pesto (or vegan pesto if desired) with a drizzle of extra-virgin olive oil, fresh lemon juice and some salt and freshly ground black pepper.

Toss the cooked spaghetti in the pesto mixture until everything is evenly coated. If the mixture looks too thick, add some starchy pasta water to thin it out.

Finally, top with a handful of arugula, some pine nuts and a pinch of red pepper flakes for an extra kick. Serve the pesto pasta warm or at room temperature - it's sure to be a hit! Enjoy!

For an even healthier version, swap out the spaghetti for your favorite whole grain variety or try zucchini noodles for a low-carb option. Top with tomatoes, olives or your favorite veggies to make it even more nutritious and tasty. Happy eating!

Tuna Pasta

Ingredients

2 tablespoons olive oil.
2 large cloves garlic minced.
1 (5 ounce) can tuna, drained I prefer tuna packed in oil.
1 teaspoon lemon juice.
1 tablespoon fresh parsley chopped.
Salt & pepper to taste.
4 ounces uncooked pasta (I used spaghetti)

Tuna pasta is a delicious and easy-to-make recipe for kids. It's perfect for busy weeknights when you don't have much time to cook. To make this delicious dish, start by heating the olive oil in a large skillet over medium heat. Add the garlic and sauté until fragrant, about 1 minute. Add the tuna and stir to combine. Then add the lemon juice and parsley, season with salt and pepper to taste, and cook for another minute or two. Finally, add the uncooked pasta to the skillet and mix everything together. Cook according to directions on the box until al dente. Serve hot and enjoy! Tuna pasta is a delicious and nutritious meal that your kids will love. Enjoy!

Mushroom Bolognese

Ingredients for Mushroom Bolognese:

2 onions, finely diced
4 large garlic cloves, chopped
2 large carrots, finely diced
2 sticks of celery, finely diced
400g mushrooms (any variety), finely chopped like mince
2 x 400g tins of whole plum tomatoes
Splash of balsamic vinegar
Glass of red wine
Salt and black pepper, to taste
Olive oil, for cooking
400g spaghetti or pasta of choice

Instructions:

Heat a generous amount of olive oil in a large saucepan over medium heat.

Add the onions and garlic, and sauté for 3-4 minutes until softened.

Add the carrots and celery, and sauté for another 5 minutes until the vegetables are slightly softened.

Add the finely chopped mushrooms to the pan, and cook for 10-15 minutes until the mushrooms have released their moisture and have browned.

Pour in the tinned plum tomatoes, using a wooden spoon to break up any large chunks.

Add a splash of balsamic vinegar and a glass of red wine to the pan.

Season with salt and black pepper to taste, and stir everything together.

Bring the sauce to a simmer and let it cook for about 30 minutes until it has thickened and the vegetables are tender.

While the sauce is cooking, cook the spaghetti in a large pot of salted boiling water according to the package instructions.

Once the spaghetti is cooked al dente, reserve a cup of the pasta cooking water and drain the spaghetti.

Add the spaghetti to the pan with the mushroom bolognese sauce and toss to coat the pasta with the sauce. If the sauce seems too thick, add a splash of the reserved pasta cooking water to loosen it up.

Serve the Mushroom Bolognese over the spaghetti, and enjoy!

Meatballs Spaghetti

Meatball spaghetti is a delicious and easy-to-make recipe for kids. This delicious dish is made with spaghetti noodles, ground beef, bread crumbs, parsley, Parmesan cheese, egg, garlic cloves, salt, red pepper flakes, extra-virgin olive oil, onion chopped finely, crushed tomatoes and one bay leaf.

To begin, cook the spaghetti noodles according to package instructions. While the pasta is cooking, prepare the meatballs: In a large bowl combine ground beef, bread crumbs, parsley, Parmesan cheese, egg and garlic cloves. Using your hands or a wooden spoon mix until everything is combined. Form into small balls about 1 inch in diameter, and set aside.

Heat a large skillet over medium heat and add the olive oil. Add the meatballs to the pan and cook until golden brown all over, about 5 minutes. Remove from the heat and set aside.

Add the onion to the same skillet over medium-high heat and sauté for 3 minutes. Add the crushed tomatoes, bay leaf and red pepper flakes and season with salt and pepper to taste. Bring to a simmer and add the cooked meatballs back into the sauce. Simmer for about 10 minutes until sauce has thickened.

Once spaghetti is done cooking, drain it and toss it in the skillet with the meatballs and sauce. Mix everything together and serve with freshly grated Parmesan cheese on top. Enjoy!

Meatball spaghetti is a delicious dish that can be enjoyed by the whole family. With its delicious combination of ingredients, it's sure to be a hit in any household! Try this delicious recipe today and enjoy delicious Italian-style food with your family and friends. Buon Appetito!

Pasta With Roasted Tomatoes And Garlic

Ingredients

1 tablespoon kosher salt
8 ounces uncooked spaghetti
¼ cup extra-virgin olive oil, divided
2 pints multicolored cherry tomatoes
4 garlic cloves, thinly sliced
½ teaspoon kosher salt
¼ teaspoon freshly ground black pepper
2 ounces Parmigiano-Reggiano cheese, shaved
¼ cup small basil leaves

Turn a regular pasta dinner into something special with this delicious and healthy dish of pasta with roasted tomatoes and garlic. The combination of colors, flavors, and textures will make it an appealing meal for kids.

To make this dish, you'll need the following ingredients: 1 tablespoon kosher salt, 8 ounces uncooked spaghetti, ¼ cup extra-virgin olive oil (divided), 2 pints multicolored cherry tomatoes, 4 garlic cloves (thinly sliced), ½ teaspoon kosher salt, ¼ teaspoon freshly ground black pepper, 2 ounces Parmigiano-Reggiano cheese (shaved), and ¼ cup small basil leaves.

To start, preheat the oven to 425°F. Place the tomatoes in a single layer on a baking sheet and sprinkle with 1 tablespoon of olive oil, the sliced garlic, ½ teaspoon kosher salt, and ¼ teaspoon freshly ground black pepper. Roast for 25 minutes until the tomatoes are lightly charred and beginning to burst open.

While the tomatoes are roasting, bring a large pot of salted water to a boil and cook the spaghetti according to package directions.

When the pasta is cooked, drain it and add the remaining olive oil. Mix in the roasted tomatoes and garlic, Parmigiano-Reggiano cheese, and fresh basil leaves. Serve hot or at room temperature for an easy and delicious meal that the kids will love. Enjoy!

Creamy Salmon Pasta

Ingredients
2 salmon fillets.
1 tbsp olive oil, plus 1 tsp if roasting.
175g penne.
2 shallots or 1 small onion, finely chopped.
1 garlic clove, crushed.
100ml white wine.
200ml double cream or crème fraîche.
¼ lemon, zested and juiced.

Creamy salmon pasta is a delicious and easy recipe for kids. This delicious meal can be prepared in just a few simple steps.

To begin, preheat your oven to 200°c (gas mark 6) and brush the salmon fillets with 1 tbsp of olive oil. Place them in the oven to bake for 12-15 minutes until cooked through. Once the salmon is cooked, flake it into small pieces and set aside.

Bring a large pot of salted water to the boil and cook your penne according to packet instructions until al dente.

Meanwhile, heat 1 tsp of olive oil in a large skillet over medium-high heat. Add the shallots or onions and garlic to the skillet and sauté for a few minutes until softened. Add the white wine, cream or crème fraîche, lemon zest, lemon juice and flaked salmon pieces. Simmer gently over low heat for around 5-7 minutes until the sauce has thickened slightly.

To serve, drain the cooked penne and combine with the sauce. Divide into plates and enjoy your delicious creamy salmon pasta!

This delicious recipe is sure to be a hit with all the family - even picky eaters will love it! With only a few simple ingredients, this meal can be prepared in no time at all so why not give it a try tonight? Enjoy!

Goat Cheese Spinach Pasta

Ingredients

8 ounces uncooked pasta.
4 ounces goat cheese crumbled.
1/2 cup freshly grated parmesan cheese.
1 teaspoon fresh lemon juice.
1 tablespoon butter.
1 clove garlic minced.
2 cups fresh baby spinach (packed)
1 tablespoon chopped fresh basil (optional)

This healthy pasta dish is easy to make and incredibly flavorful. It combines the tangy flavor of goat cheese with the earthy taste of spinach, all tossed in a light lemon butter sauce.

To prepare, begin by bringing a pot of salted water to a boil over high heat. Add the pasta and cook for 8-10 minutes until al dente.

Meanwhile, melt the butter in a large skillet over medium heat. Add the garlic and sauté for one minute, then reduce the heat to low and add the spinach. Cook until wilted and tender, about 3-4 minutes.

Add the cooked pasta to the skillet with the spinach, stirring to combine. Add the goat cheese and parmesan, stirring until melted. Finally, stir in the lemon juice and season with salt, pepper, and fresh basil (if using). Serve warm.

This healthy pasta dish is a great way to get your dose of greens while still indulging in comfort food. Enjoy!

Penne Arrabiata

Ingredients
6 tablespoons extra virgin olive oil, plus extra for cooking the pasta
2 medium hot chilies, finely sliced
2 garlic cloves, chopped
Handful of basil leaves
600g/1lb 5oz canned chopped tomatoes
Salt, to taste
400g/14oz fresh penne pasta
Parmesan shavings (or similar vegetarian hard cheese), to serve

Instructions:

Heat the olive oil in a large saucepan over medium heat.

Add the sliced chilies and chopped garlic to the pan and sauté for 1-2 minutes, stirring frequently, until the garlic is fragrant.

Add the canned chopped tomatoes to the pan and bring to a simmer. Cook the sauce for 10-15 minutes, stirring occasionally, until it has thickened slightly.

While the sauce is cooking, bring a large pot of salted water to a boil. Add the fresh penne pasta and cook according to package instructions until al dente.

Reserve a cup of the pasta cooking water and then drain the penne.

Add the cooked penne to the saucepan with the arrabiata sauce and toss well to coat the pasta in the sauce. If the sauce seems too thick, add a splash of the reserved pasta cooking water to loosen it up.

Season the Penne Arrabiata with salt to taste.

Serve the Penne Arrabiata in bowls, topped with fresh basil leaves and Parmesan shavings. Enjoy!

Pasta Salad

Ingredients

1 pound tri-colored spiral pasta
1 (16 ounce) bottle Italian-style salad dressing
6 tablespoons salad seasoning mix (or a mixture of dried oregano, basil, thyme, and garlic powder)
2 cups cherry tomatoes, diced
1 green bell pepper, chopped
1 red bell pepper, diced
1/2 yellow bell pepper, chopped
1 (2.25 ounce) can black olives, chopped

Instructions:

Cook the pasta according to package instructions until al dente. Drain the pasta and rinse with cold water to stop the cooking process. Drain the pasta again and set aside.

In a large bowl, whisk together the Italian-style salad dressing and salad seasoning mix.

Add the cooked pasta, cherry tomatoes, bell peppers, and black olives to the bowl with the dressing. Toss well to coat everything evenly.

Cover the bowl with plastic wrap and refrigerate for at least 1 hour to let the flavors meld together.

When ready to serve, give the pasta salad a good stir and adjust the seasoning if necessary. Add additional salad dressing if the pasta seems dry.

Serve the Pasta Salad chilled, garnished with fresh herbs or grated Parmesan cheese, if desired. Enjoy!

Carbonara Spaghetti

Carbonara spaghetti is a delicious recipe for kids to learn how to cook. The ingredients you will need are 100g of pancetta, 50g of pecorino cheese, 50g of parmesan, 3 large eggs, 350g of spaghetti, 2 plump garlic cloves (peeled and left whole), 50g unsalted butter, sea salt, and freshly ground black pepper. To begin cooking this delicious dish, bring a large saucepan of salted water to the boil. Add the spaghetti and cook until al dente (around 8-10 minutes). Meanwhile, fry the pancetta in a dry non-stick frying pan over moderate heat for about 5 minutes until lightly golden. Once cooked, set aside and keep warm. In a small bowl, mix together the pecorino cheese and parmesan with the eggs until you have a creamy sauce. Season well with salt and pepper. When the spaghetti is cooked, drain it, reserving some of the cooking water. Add the spaghetti to the pan with the pancetta and garlic, and stir everything together. Add the butter, stirring until melted. Pour over the egg mixture and toss everything together well with a little of the reserved cooking water - this will help to make it nice and creamy. Serve immediately while still warm. Enjoy!

This delicious carbonara spaghetti dish is sure to be a hit with the whole family. With just a few ingredients and simple steps, your kids can learn to make this delicious dinner in no time! Serve it with a fresh salad on the side for a delicious meal that everyone will love. Enjoy!

Ravioli Lasagna

This delicious ravioli lasagna recipe is sure to be a hit with kids and adults alike! To make this delicious dish, you will need 1 pound of ground beef, 1 jar (28 ounces) spaghetti sauce, 1 package (25 ounces) frozen sausage or cheese ravioli, 1-1/2 cups shredded part-skim mozzarella cheese and minced fresh basil (optional).

Begin by cooking the ground beef in a large skillet over medium-high heat until no longer pink, stirring occasionally. Drain off any fat. Add spaghetti sauce to the cooked beef and bring mixture to a boil. Reduce heat; simmer for about 10 minutes or until heated through, stirring occasionally.

Meanwhile, cook ravioli according to package directions. Drain and set aside. Preheat oven to 350°F (175°C). In a greased 13x9-inch baking dish, layer one-third of the beef mixture, half of the cooked ravioli, and one-third of the cheese. Repeat layers. Top with remaining beef mixture and cheese.

Bake, uncovered, for 25 to 30 minutes or until bubbly and cheese is melted. If desired, sprinkle with basil before serving. Enjoy! With a few simple ingredients, this delicious recipe makes an easy meal that the whole family will love! Try it today for a delicious meal that will keep the kids asking for more. Bon Appétit!

Spinach Mascarpone Lasagne

Ingredients
400g spinach.
1 tbsp olive oil.
2 garlic cloves, crushed.
250g mascarpone.
1 tsp ground nutmeg.
100g parmesan (or vegetarian alternative), grated.
9 lasagne sheets.
100ml double cream.

This healthy spinach and mascarpone lasagne is a delicious pasta dish that's easy to prepare. Start by preheating the oven to 200C/180C fan/gas 6. Then, heat 1 tablespoon of olive oil in a large saucepan over medium heat. Add 2 crushed garlic cloves and 400g of spinach, stirring until wilted.

In a separate bowl, combine 250g of mascarpone and 1 teaspoon of ground nutmeg. Then layer the lasagne sheets in an ovenproof dish, alternating with spoonfuls of the spinach and mascarpone mixture, plus 100 millilitres of double cream. Sprinkle over 100 grams of grated parmesan or a suitable vegetarian alternative.

Bake in the oven for 25 minutes until golden and bubbling. Serve with a side salad and enjoy! You can also freeze any leftovers, making this healthy spinach and mascarpone lasagne perfect for busy weeknights. Enjoy!

Pasta Bolognese

Ingredients

1 tbsp olive oil.
4 rashers smoked streaky bacon, finely chopped.
2 medium onions, finely chopped.
2 carrots, trimmed and finely chopped.
2 celery sticks, finely chopped.
2 garlic cloves finely chopped.
2-3 sprigs rosemary leaves picked and finely chopped.
500g beef mince.

Pasta bolognese is one of those delicious recipes that kids will love. And it's a great way to introduce them to cooking at home. Here's how to make it:

Start by heating the olive oil in a large saucepan over medium heat. Add the bacon, onions, carrots and celery sticks and cook, stirring regularly, for about 5 minutes. Next, add the garlic and rosemary leaves and cook for a further 2 minutes.

Add the mince to the pan, breaking it up with a wooden spoon as it cooks. Cook until browned all over, then reduce heat and simmer for 10-15 minutes.

Finally, add the tomato puree and season to taste. Cook for a further 10 minutes or until thickened then serve with your favorite pasta. Enjoy!

This delicious pasta bolognese dish is sure to be loved by kids and adults alike. With just a few simple ingredients, it's easy to make and can be on the dinner table in just under 30 minutes. So the next time you need a delicious and family-friendly meal, try out this delicious pasta bolognese!

Bon Appetite!

Cheesy Tortellini

Ingredients

2 cups cheese tortellini (fresh or frozen)
2 tablespoons salted butter.
2 cloves freshly minced garlic.
¼ teaspoon Italian seasoning.
¼ teaspoon salt.
freshly cracked pepper.
½ cup heavy cream.
2 tablespoons freshly grated Parmesan cheese.

Cheesy tortellini is a healthy and delicious pasta dish that can be prepared in just minutes. To make it, start by cooking the cheese tortellini according to the instructions on the package. Once cooked, set aside and melt butter in a large skillet over medium-high heat. Add garlic, Italian seasoning, salt, and pepper and sauté for 1-2 minutes until fragrant. Add the heavy cream to the skillet and bring to a simmer. Lastly, add the cooked tortellini and Parmesan cheese to the skillet and gently stir everything together until combined. Serve warm with extra Parmesan cheese on top if desired! Enjoy!

This cheesy tortellini dish is an easy yet healthy meal that the whole family will love. Make it for a weeknight dinner or a special occasion - either way, you're sure to have a winning dish on your hands! Enjoy!

Pasta With Salmon And Peas

Looking for delicious recipes that are perfect for kids? This delicious pasta dish with salmon and peas is a great option. Not only is it easy to make, but it's packed full of flavour and packed full of protein and other essential nutrients. To make this delicious recipe, you will need the following ingredients: 240g wholewheat fusilli, a knob of butter, 1 large shallot finely chopped, 140g frozen peas, 2 skinless salmon fillets cut into chunks, 140g low-fat crème fraîche, ½ low-salt vegetable stock cube and a small bunch of chives snipped.

To begin, heat the butter in a large pan over a medium heat. Once melted, add the shallot and cook until softened for about 3 minutes. Then add the peas and salmon chunks, cook for 2 minutes, stirring constantly. Add the crème fraîche and stock cube to the pan and stir everything together until combined. Finally, add the fusilli to the pan and mix everything together. Cook for 8-10 minutes, stirring often.

Once the fusilli is cooked and all of the ingredients are combined, sprinkle over the chives and serve. Your delicious pasta dish with salmon and peas is now ready to be enjoyed by your family! Enjoy!

Cheesy Broccoli Pasta

Ingredients
½ cup butter.
1 onion, chopped. Fresh Onions.
1 (16 ounce) package frozen chopped broccoli.
4 (14.5 ounce) cans chicken broth.
1 (1 pound) loaf processed cheese food, cubed.
2 cups milk.
1 tablespoon garlic powder.
⅔ cup cornstarch.

This delicious cheesy broccoli pasta is a sure hit for kids and adults alike! With just a few simple steps, anyone can make this delicious dish in no time.

First, melt the butter in a large pot over medium heat. Add the chopped onion and cook until softened, about 5 minutes. Next, add the frozen chopped broccoli and chicken broth and bring to a boil. Reduce the heat, cover, and simmer for 15 minutes.

Once done, add the cubed cheese food, milk, garlic powder and cornstarch to the pot. Give it all a good stir then cover and cook for about 10 more minutes or until the sauce has thickened. Serve hot with your favorite sides!

This cheesy broccoli pasta is delicious and easy to make, making it an ideal recipe for kids. If you're looking for a delicious and nutritious dish that your whole family can enjoy, this is the perfect choice! So what are you waiting for? Try out this delicious cheesy broccoli pasta today!

Enjoy

Shrimps Alfredo Pasta

Shrimp Alfredo pasta is a delicious and easy recipe to make for kids. It's quick, delicious, and full of flavor! To start, you'll need to gather all the necessary ingredients: Fettuccine pasta, shrimp (I used frozen raw 31-40 count per pound size shrimp; you can use smaller or larger), butter (unsalted), cream cheese (for added texture and tangy taste), heavy cream, chicken broth (for added flavor), garlic, and Parmesan cheese.

Once you have all of the ingredients ready to go, start by cooking the fettuccine pasta according to package instructions. Once cooked, drain and set aside. In a large skillet or pan, heat butter over medium-high heat. Add the shrimp to the skillet and cook for 3-5 minutes or until they turn pink. Next, add in the garlic and sauté for 2 minutes. Add in cream cheese, heavy cream, and chicken broth and mix everything together until well combined. Lastly, add in the cooked fettuccine pasta and stir for 1-2 minutes until everything is well incorporated. Serve the delicious Shrimp Alfredo pasta with a generous helping of freshly grated Parmesan cheese. Enjoy!

This delicious Shrimp Alfredo pasta recipe is sure to please the whole family, kids included! It's an easy and delicious way to show your family how much you care. Plus, it's a great way to teach kids how to cook delicious recipes for themselves. So what are you waiting for? Give this delicious Shrimp Alfredo pasta recipe a try today!

Seafood Pasta

Ingredients

1 lb (454 g) scallops, fresh or thawed.
Kosher salt.
12 oz (340 g) good quality pasta.
3 Tbsp extra virgin olive oil.
8 large or 12 medium raw shrimp, fresh or frozen (and thawed) peeled, and deveined.
3 or 4 cloves minced garlic.
chopped Italian, flat leaf parsley.
freshly ground black pepper.

Seafood pasta is a delicious and easy-to-make meal that kids of all ages can enjoy. To prepare this delicious dish, start by bringing a pot of salted water to a boil before adding the pasta. Cook it until just al dente, then drain it and set aside.

In a large skillet over medium heat, heat the olive oil and garlic until fragrant. Add the scallops and shrimp, season with salt and pepper, and cook for 3-4 minutes or until cooked through. Add the cooked pasta to the skillet along with fresh parsley, and stir to combine everything together.

Serve your delicious seafood pasta in individual bowls accompanied by a side salad and delicious garlic bread. It's a delicious meal that kids are sure to love, and it's a great way to introduce them to the joys of cooking!
Enjoy!

Spaghetti Alla Norma

Ingredients

2 aubergines (eggplants), cut into small cubes
3 cloves of garlic, minced
1/2 bunch of fresh basil (about 15g), finely chopped
1 teaspoon dried oregano
1 teaspoon dried chili flakes
Olive oil, for cooking
1 tablespoon baby capers
1 tablespoon red wine vinegar
1 x 400g can of quality plum tomatoes, crushed or pureed
320g dried wholewheat spaghetti
50g pecorino cheese, grated
Extra-virgin olive oil, for serving

Instructions:

Preheat your oven to 200°C (180°C fan)/400°F/gas 6.

Spread the cubed aubergines in a single layer on a baking tray, drizzle with olive oil and sprinkle with salt. Roast for 20-25 minutes until golden and tender.

In a large pan, heat 2-3 tablespoons of olive oil over medium heat. Add the minced garlic, dried oregano, and dried chili flakes, and cook for a minute until fragrant.

Add the baby capers and red wine vinegar to the pan and cook for another minute.

Pour in the crushed/pureed plum tomatoes and stir to combine with the garlic mixture. Bring the sauce to a simmer and let it cook for 10-15 minutes, stirring occasionally.

Cook the spaghetti according to the package instructions until al dente.

Drain the spaghetti, reserving 1/2 cup of the pasta cooking water.

Add the cooked spaghetti to the tomato sauce and toss to combine. If the sauce seems too thick, add a splash of the reserved pasta cooking water to loosen it up.

Add the roasted aubergines to the pan with the spaghetti and tomato sauce, and stir to combine.

Serve the Spaghetti alla Norma hot, topped with grated pecorino cheese and fresh chopped basil. Drizzle with extra-virgin olive oil before serving. Enjoy!

Chickpea Pasta

Ingredients:

8 ounces rotini chickpea pasta
2 tablespoons olive oil
1-15 ounce can chickpeas, drained and rinsed
3 garlic cloves, minced
1/4 teaspoon red pepper flakes
1 teaspoon kosher salt
1/2 teaspoon black pepper
Juice and zest of 1 lemon

Instructions:

Cook the pasta in a large pot of salted boiling water according to package directions until al dente. Drain and set aside.

While the pasta is cooking, heat the olive oil in a large skillet over medium heat. Add the chickpeas and cook for 3-4 minutes, stirring occasionally, until lightly browned and crispy.

Add the garlic, red pepper flakes, salt, and black pepper to the skillet and cook for another 1-2 minutes, stirring frequently, until fragrant.

Add the cooked pasta to the skillet and toss with the chickpeas and seasonings. Add the lemon juice and zest and toss again until everything is well combined.

Serve the pasta hot, garnished with additional lemon zest and chopped parsley or basil, if desired.

Enjoy your delicious and healthy chickpea pasta!

Easy Pesto Lasagne

Ingredients

190g jar pesto
500g tub mascarpone
200g bag spinach, roughly chopped
250g frozen pea
small pack basil, leaves chopped, and a few leaves reserved to finish
small pack mint, leaves chopped
12 fresh lasagne sheets
splash of milk
85g parmesan, grated (or vegetarian alternative)
50g pine nuts
green salad, to serve (optional)

This delicious pesto lasagne is an easy way to please even the pickiest eaters! Perfect for a weeknight dinner, this recipe is simple to make and full of delicious flavors. To begin, preheat your oven to 200 degrees Celsius (400 degrees Fahrenheit).

In a large bowl, stir together the jar of pesto, the mascarpone, chopped spinach, frozen peas, chopped basil, and chopped mint. Once combined, set aside.

In a large ovenproof dish, spread a layer of the pesto mixture on the bottom. Top with 3 lasagne sheets. Spread another layer of the pesto mixture over the top and sprinkle with parmesan or vegetarian alternative. Sprinkle with pine nuts and top with 3 more lasagne sheets.

Continue layering up the dish in this way, finishing with a layer of pesto mixture and parmesan. Pour over a splash of milk and sprinkle over some extra chopped basil leaves. Bake in the preheated oven for 25 minutes, until golden and bubbling.

This delicious pesto lasagne is a great recipe for kids to try their hand at cooking - sure to be a hit with the whole family! Serve warm with a green salad, if desired. Enjoy!

Baked Feta Pasta

ingredients

2 pints (20 oz) grape tomatoes.
1/2 cup extra-virgin olive oil.
Salt and freshly ground black pepper.
7 oz. block feta cheese (sheep's milk variety), drained.
10 oz. dry pasta (bite size)
5 medium garlic cloves, peeled and halved.
8 oz. ...
1/4 tsp crushed red pepper flakes, or more to taste.

Baked Feta Pasta is an easy and healthy dish that takes only minimal time to prepare. With just a handful of simple ingredients, you can create this delicious meal. To make it, start by preheating your oven to 425 degrees Fahrenheit.

In a large bowl, combine the grape tomatoes, extra-virgin olive oil, salt and pepper. Cut the feta cheese into small cubes and add it to the bowl. Next, cook 10 oz of bite-size pasta according to package instructions until al dente. Once done, drain it and mix it with the tomato mixture in the bowl.

Add garlic cloves, 8 oz of mushrooms (sliced), and 1/4 tsp of crushed red pepper flakes, or to taste. Toss everything together and spread it in a single layer on an oven-safe dish. Bake for 25 minutes until the top is lightly golden brown.

Baked Feta Pasta is now ready to enjoy! Serve with a sprinkling of fresh herbs, extra olive oil, and a side of crusty bread. This healthy pasta dish makes for a great weeknight dinner that is sure to please the whole family.
Enjoy!

Cottage Cheese Alfredo

This healthy cottage cheese alfredo pasta is a delicious and easy weeknight dinner. It's made with simple ingredients and comes together in no time! Using plain or chive-flavored cottage cheese gives the creamy sauce its unique flavor, while frozen peas add texture and sweetness. Spaghetti or linguini both work well for this recipe. To begin, cook the pasta according to package directions. While the pasta is cooking, heat a large skillet over medium-high heat and add a tablespoon of olive oil. Add minced garlic and cook for 1 minute, or until fragrant. Then stir in cottage cheese and 1/4 cup reserved pasta water (or more if needed). Season with salt and pepper to taste. Reduce heat to low and stir until the cheese is melted and the sauce is creamy. Add cooked pasta, frozen peas, and freshly grated Parmesan cheese and stir to combine. Serve warm with extra Parmesan cheese on top if desired. Enjoy! This healthy cottage cheese alfredo pasta dish is sure to become a family favorite. With its creamy sauce and flavorful additions, it's a healthy twist on classic Italian cuisine. Enjoy!

This healthy cottage cheese alfredo pasta dish is an easy to make weeknight dinner that will delight the entire family. Start by cooking the pasta according to package directions and set aside 1/4 cup of reserved water. Heat a large skillet over medium-high heat and add a tablespoon of olive oil. Add minced garlic and cook for 1 minute, or until fragrant. Then stir in cottage cheese and reserved pasta water (or more if needed). Season with salt and pepper to taste. Reduce heat to low and stir until the cheese is melted and the sauce is creamy. Add cooked pasta, frozen peas, and freshly grated Parmesan cheese and stir to combine. Serve warm with extra Parmesan cheese on top if desired. Enjoy! This healthy cottage cheese alfredo pasta dish is a great way to enjoy Italian flavors in a healthy way. With its creamy sauce and flavorful additions, it's sure to become a family favorite. Enjoy!

Creamy Chicken Pasta

Ingredients
500 g | 1lb large chicken breasts (or skinless boneless thighs)
Salt and pepper , to season.
1/2 tbsp olive oil , to fry the chicken.
1 tbsp unsalted butter.
3 garlic cloves , minced.
500 ml | 2 cups double / heavy cream (or you can use single cream)
50 g | ½ cup freshly grated Parmesan cheese.
1 tsp salt.

For delicious recipes for kids, try this Creamy Chicken Pasta! It's easy to make and takes less than 30 minutes. Start by seasoning the chicken breasts with salt and pepper. Heat oil in a large skillet over medium-high heat, then add the chicken breast. Cook until it turns golden brown on both sides, about 4 minutes per side. Once cooked, remove the chicken and set aside. In the same pan, melt butter over medium heat and add minced garlic. Cook for 1 minute until fragrant. Pour in the cream and bring it to a simmer before adding Parmesan cheese and salt. Stir everything together until combined, then add the cooked chicken back in the pan. Reduce heat to low and simmer for 10 minutes, stirring occasionally. Serve over cooked pasta of your choice and enjoy! With this delicious recipe, you can easily delight even the pickiest of eaters. Bon appetite!

Spaghetti Alla Putanesca

Ingredients

400 grams of spaghetti
100 grams of pitted olives
1 tablespoon salted capers
500 grams of well-ripened tomatoes or 400 grams of tomatoes in broth
2 large garlic cloves
5-6 anchovy fillets salted or in oil
1 sprig parsley
3-4 tablespoons olive oil
salt and pepper
optional: chilli pepper, fresh or dried

If you're looking for delicious recipes for kids, look no further than spaghetti alla Puttanesca. This classic Italian dish is easy to make and packed with flavour. Here's how to cook it:

Firstly, bring a large pot of salted water to a rolling boil and add the 400 grams of spaghetti. Cook until al dente, then strain and set aside.

In a large skillet over medium heat, add the 3-4 tablespoons of olive oil and two large cloves of garlic, chopped. When the garlic begins to sizzle, stir for about 30 seconds before adding anchovy fillets salted or in oil. Stir until the anchovies have dissolved into the oil.

Now you can add the pitted olives and capers, stirring for another 1-2 minutes before adding 500 grams of well-ripened tomatoes or 400 grams of tomatoes in broth. Season with salt and pepper to taste, plus chilli pepper if desired. Simmer for about 10 minutes until all the flavours have combined.

Finally, add the strained spaghetti and stir for 1-2 minutes to ensure everything is well mixed together. Serve in bowls with freshly chopped parsley as a garnish. Enjoy!

I want to take a moment to express my heartfelt gratitude for your recent purchase of my recipe book. As a passionate food lover, nothing makes me happier than sharing my favorite recipes with others. Your decision to invest in my book not only supports my dream, but also shows your commitment to expanding your culinary horizons.

I sincerely hope that the recipes in the book will inspire you to try new things and add some excitement to your meals.

Thank you again for your support and for being a part of this journey with me. I hope my book will bring you many happy and delicious moments in the kitchen.

www.ingramcontent.com/pod-product-compliance
Lightning Source LLC
Chambersburg PA
CBHW041150110526
44590CB00027B/4185